Collins FLAGSHIP HISTORYMAKERS

CROMWELL

ELIZABETH SPAREY

D0795300

An imprint of HarperCollins*Publishers*

Pub
77–85 Fulham
London
W6 8JB

Browse the complete Collins catalogue at
www.collinseducation.com

British Library Cataloguing in Publication Data. A
catalogue record for this book is available from the
British Library.

Series commissioned by Graham Bradbury
Project management by Will Chuter
Edited by Sue Chapple
Design by Derek Lee
Picture research by Celia Dearing
Production by Sarah Robinson
Printed and bound by Printing Express Ltd.,
Hong Kong

...MENTS

..?ublishers would like to thank the following
for permission to reproduce extracts from their
books:

Blackwell for the extract from *Cromwell and the
Interregnum* by David Smith (2003). Hodder
Arnold for the extract from *Oliver Cromwell* by J. C.
Davis (2001). Penguin Books for the extract from
Stuart England by J. P. Kenyon (1985).

The Publishers would like to thank the following
for permission to reproduce pictures on these pages
T=Top, B=Bottom, L=Left, R=Right, C=Centre

Akg images-London 35; www.bridgeman.co.uk
/©Lady Lever Art Gallery, Port Sunlight,
Merseyside, National Museums Liverpool *Cromwell
on his Farm,* 1874 4 (oil on canvas) by Ford
Maddox Brown 9, www.bridgeman.co.uk/Private
Collection/Ken Welsh 20,
www.bridgeman.co.uk/Private Collection *The
Emblem of England's Distractions,* 1658 27,
www.bridgeman.co.uk/Private Collection miniature
of Oliver Cromwell by Samuel Cooper 29,
www.bridgeman.co.uk/ Private Collection 53, 55;
©Historical Picture Archive/Corbis 7; The Fotomas
Index 43; Getty Images/Hulton Archive 8, 15, 19,
21, 25, 37, 45, 61; Mary Evans Picture Library 32,
34; The National Portrait Gallery, London, John
Lambert *c.*1650–1655 (oil on canvas) after Robert
Walker 14; The Royal Collection © 2004, Her
Majesty Queen Elizabeth II, *Charles I at his Trial,*
by Edward Bower 12.

Cover picture: portrait of Oliver Cromwell, English
school, seventeenth century, Private
Collection/www.bridgeman.co.uk

Every effort has been made to contact the holders
of copyright material, but if any have been
inadvertently overlooked the Publishers will be
pleased to make the necessary arrangements at the
first opportunity.

You might also like to visit
www.harpercollins.co.uk
The book lovers' website

Contents

Why do historians differ?

THE purpose of the Flagship Historymakers series is to explore the main debates surrounding a number of key individuals in British, European and American History.

Each book begins with a chronology of the significant events in the life of the particular individual, and an outline of the person's career. The book then examines in greater detail three of the most important and controversial issues in the life of the individual – issues which continue to attract differing views from historians, and which feature prominently in examination syllabuses in A-level History and beyond.

Each of these issue sections provides students with an overview of the main arguments put forward by historians. By posing key questions, these sections aim to help students to think through the areas of debate and to form their own judgements on the evidence. It is important, therefore, for students to understand why historians differ in their views on past events and, in particular, on the role of individuals in past events.

The study of history is an ongoing debate about events in the past. Although factual evidence is the essential ingredient of history, it is the *interpretation* of factual evidence that forms the basis for historical debate. The study of how and why historians differ in their various interpretations is termed 'historiography'.

Historical debate can occur for a wide variety of reasons.

Insufficient evidence

In some cases there is insufficient evidence to provide a definitive conclusion. In attempting to 'fill the gaps' where factual evidence is unavailable, historians use their professional judgement to make 'informed comments' about the past.

New evidence

As new evidence comes to light, an historian today may have more information on which to base judgements than historians in the past. For instance, the County Record Offices provide a wealth of documentary evidence showing how government policies, including those of the seventeenth century, were carried out locally. As more of this evidence is examined and analysed by historians, conclusions about the nature and impact of central government can be re-assessed.

A 'philosophy' of history?

Many historians have a specific view of history that will affect the way they make their historical judgements. For instance, Marxist historians – who take their view from the writings of Karl Marx, the founder of modern socialism – believe that society has always been made up of competing economic and social classes. They also place considerable importance on economic reasons behind human decision-making. Therefore, a Marxist historian looking at an historical issue may take a completely different viewpoint to a non-Marxist historian.

The role of the individual

Some historians have seen past history as being largely moulded by the acts of specific individuals. Charles I and Oliver Cromwell are seen as individuals whose personality and beliefs changed the course of seventeenth-century British history. Other historians have tended to play down the role of individuals; instead, they highlight the importance of more general social, economic, political and ideological change. Rather than seeing John Pym as an individual who changed the course of political history, these historians tend to see him as representing the views of a broader group of individuals, such as the Puritan gentry of mid-seventeenth century England.

Placing different emphasis on the same historical evidence

Even if historians do not possess different philosophies of history or place different emphasis on the role of the individual, it is still possible for them to disagree in one very important way. This is that they may place different emphases on aspects of the same factual evidence. As a result, History should be seen as a subject that encourages debate about the past, based on historical evidence.

Historians will always differ

Historical debate is, in its nature, continuous. What today may be an accepted view about a past event may well change in the future, as the debate continues.

Timeline: Cromwell's life

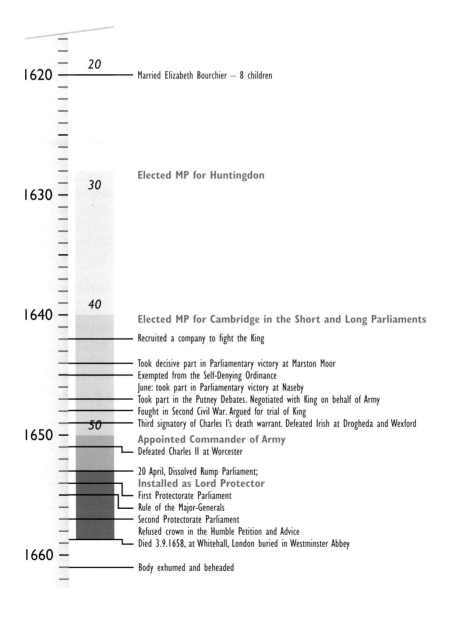

1600 — *age* — Born 25.4.1599, Huntingdon
Educated at Huntingdon Grammar School
Cambridge (Sidney Sussex)

1620 — 20 — Married Elizabeth Bourchier — 8 children

Elected MP for Huntingdon

1630 — 30

1640 — 40 — **Elected MP for Cambridge in the Short and Long Parliaments**

Recruited a company to fight the King

Took decisive part in Parliamentary victory at Marston Moor
Exempted from the Self-Denying Ordinance
June: took part in Parliamentary victory at Naseby
Took part in the Putney Debates. Negotiated with King on behalf of Army
Fought in Second Civil War. Argued for trial of King
50 — Third signatory of Charles I's death warrant. Defeated Irish at Drogheda and Wexford

1650 — **Appointed Commander of Army**
Defeated Charles II at Worcester

20 April, Dissolved Rump Parliament;
Installed as Lord Protector
First Protectorate Parliament
Rule of the Major-Generals
Second Protectorate Parliament
Refused crown in the Humble Petition and Advice
Died 3.9.1658, at Whitehall, London buried in Westminster Abbey

1660 —
Body exhumed and beheaded

VARIVS CROMWELL EXERCITVVM ANGLIÆ. REIPVBLICÆ DVX GENERALIS, LOCVM-
ENENS ET GVBERNATOR HIBERNIÆ OXO NIENSIS ACADEMIÆ CANCELLARIVS

Cernimus hic omni Caput admirabile Mundo; Nullus Ille timet quàm Summi Numinis arma
Quod Reges, Populi, Barbariesq; stupent Non timet; at Pacem Cuilibet ense parat.
Regibus Hic Frater, Populis Pater, Hostis, multam Quis dubitat Sacro hoc si pergat Flamine Victor,
Barbariem vera Relligione domat.

Cromwell depicted in civilian clothes, shortly after his triumphant return to London from Ireland. The dark clouds behind him, that represent difficulties, have broken to bathe him in victorious sunlight.

Oliver Cromwell: a brief biography

How did he make history?

OLIVER CROMWELL (1599–1658) was at the centre of a unique set of events in English, and indeed British, history. In the 2002 BBC television series, Cromwell was voted among the top ten Great Britons. In his programme on Cromwell, broadcaster Richard Holmes explained that he judged Cromwell to be the greatest Briton because, 'when Britain stood on the edge of anarchy he emerged from obscurity to help give us parliamentary democracy – our proudest achievement'. This is the popular view, yet it is one that many would not regard as historically accurate. Cromwell has been studied and argued about ever since he came to prominence during the 1640s. Every year more articles and books are published about him and, as the historian David Smith recently wrote in *Cromwell and the Interregnum* (2003), 'the period will lose neither its power to fascinate, excite and disturb, nor its compelling claim to be studied'.

The Obscure Country Gentleman

Oliver Cromwell was born in 1599 in Huntingdon, East Anglia, the eldest surviving son of the family. His father was comfortably off, but not wealthy, with an annual income of about £300. The family was, however, well connected. Oliver's father was the younger son of a knight. This put them in the class of the **lesser gentry**.

Lesser gentry: the gentry was the class immediately below the aristocracy, which consisted of gentlemen of good breeding.

For the first forty-three years of his life, Cromwell was not a figure of national importance. He was educated at the local grammar school and at Sidney Sussex College, Cambridge. In 1617 he left without graduating because his father had died, leaving Oliver as head of a family in reduced circumstances. He then spent three years studying in London, perhaps at one of the Inns of Court, although no records survive, with a view to becoming a lawyer. In 1621 he married Elizabeth Bourchier, the daughter of a London fur dealer with connections among the gentry of Essex. The marriage was a happy one and the Cromwells produced eight children.

For the following decade he lived in Huntingdon, where he probably took part in local government. There

Elizabeth Bourchier

This 1874 painting shows Cromwell at his farm at St Ives. He is shown as having close links with the ordinary people of England, and is deep in thought. He is holding a book — probably the Bible — and a branch of oak, symbolising England.

are insufficient records to be sure of his role, if any. Certainly, he was one of Huntingdon's MPs in the 1628 Parliament, which suggests that he was a prominent local figure. However, he is only recorded as having made one speech, so was not a significant figure in Parliament.

It has been claimed that about this time he suffered a nervous breakdown and underwent a religious conversion to a more Puritanical form of Protestantism. In 1631, he sold most of his land and moved five miles east to St. Ives. There, he made a living as a **yeoman** farmer. His social and economic standing had taken a turn for the worse. In 1636 his fortunes revived when an uncle left him rights on lands which brought an annual income of about £300 by 1641.

Yeoman: a prosperous farmer who worked the land himself.

From MP to regicide

Freeman: an inhabitant of a town or city who had political rights in that place.

Early in 1640 he was made a **freeman** of Cambridge. This enabled him to be elected an MP for that town a few months later in the

Short Parliament which met for three weeks in May 1640. He was re-elected, to the Long Parliament which met in November 1640. It is possible that his Puritan socio-religious circle helped to engineer his election in a town where he can have had few contacts. Certainly the election of an outsider as an MP for Cambridge was most unusual.

Still Cromwell did not emerge into the limelight. However, he did sit on a number of important parliamentary committees. As the tension between King and Parliament mounted, and divisions widened between groups of MPs, he was increasingly noticed. Cromwell was thoroughly committed to the 'revolutionary' party which demanded further concessions from the King after the summer of 1641. His plain-spoken manner was now more in tune with the mood of those MPs who did not trust the King. As war became imminent in the summer of 1642, Cromwell returned to East Anglia to raise men for Parliament's Army. His first notable action was to prevent college plate from Cambridge making its way into the King's coffers.

Cromwell now made his name as a cavalry officer in the Parliamentary Army in the First Civil War of 1642–1646. He played a critical part in military successes, such as Marston Moor and Naseby, where his tight control of his men was integral to victory. He was also respected by his men for ensuring that they were regularly paid, and for his insistence on moral and spiritual discipline. He famously said that belief in the parliamentary cause was more important than social standing when choosing Army officers.

Limited monarchy: a monarchy in which the King's power is shared with Parliament.

When the First Civil War was won, Cromwell, one of only a very few MPs in the Army, became involved in negotiations with the King. The aim was to create a **limited monarchy**. When dissent began to emerge between Army and Parliament and within Parliament about what political and religious form the settlement would take, Cromwell acted as an **arbiter**. However, by 1647 it was becoming clear to him that Charles was not to be trusted and perhaps should be removed. Charles's dealings with the Scots, which brought about the Second Civil War, confirmed this. By late 1648, Cromwell was speaking in favour of putting the King on trial for treason, and his is the third signature on the King's death warrant.

Arbiter: someone who tries to negotiate a deal between two sides.

From Army Commander to Lord Protector

Rump Parliament: a term referring to the MPs who sat from 6 December 1648 until April 1653. These MPs were recalled by the Army in 1659.

With the King dead, and control now in the hands of **The Rump Parliament** and the Council of State (Cromwell was a member of both), Cromwell's next mission was to subdue the enemies of the

Understanding Cromwell

Cromwell presents a number of contradictory impressions, which can nevertheless be reconciled:

- **A brilliant military leader**, who did not take up arms until he was in his forties.

- **A well-educated man**, who knew the Bible in great detail, yet showed no sign of being widely-read.

- **A political leader**, but one who never made reference to works of political theory in his speeches.

- **A man who reflected deeply before making decisions**, yet sometimes acted impulsively.

- **A believer in parliamentary government**, who expelled a parliament and established a regime dependent on military support.

- **A religious radical**, but political conservative.

- **A regicide**, who seriously considered accepting the crown.

- **A merciful man**, but who had the Leveller leaders shot and allowed thousands of Irish to be displaced from their land.

- **A man who believed in justice for all**, yet who denied a fair trial to those who opposed his regime.

- **A man who believed in promotion on merit**, yet whose family played a prominent part in his regime.

- **A man of simple pleasures**, who lived in a king's palace and was addressed as 'Your Highness'.

- **A deeply religious, Christian man**, who banned the celebration of Christmas.

> *'He will be looked upon by posterity as a brave bad man.'*
> Edward Hyde, Earl of Clarendon

Charles I at his trial. The King was at his most dignified and composed at his trial in January 1649, losing the stammer that made effective communication difficult for him. However, since he refused to recognise the authority of he court and its right to try him, he was sent away while the evidence was heard, only returning to hear the verdict and sentence.

Commonwealth: a form of government in which the power rests with the people rather than with a hereditary Head of State.

Levellers: a radical religious and political group, influential in the Parliamentary Army in the late 1640s.

new **Commonwealth**. First were his former associates in the Army, the **Levellers**. Mutinous Leveller troops were suppressed and the ringleaders shot. Here, as in many other circumstances, the issue of Cromwell's consistency is in question. After this Cromwell, now commander-in-chief of the Parliamentary Army, took his army to Ireland then Scotland to bring the two countries under English control. His actions in Ireland have proved to be among the most controversial in his career. In 1651, having successfully completed these tasks from a military point of view, he returned to London, never to lead an army in the field again.

Cromwell spent the last seven years of his life as a politician, though retaining strong links with the Army. With the Rump

Charles I (1600–49)

The story of Oliver Cromwell is inevitably closely intertwined with the story of the King he helped to overthrow. Charles was born in Scotland and was such a weakly child that he was temporarily left in Scotland when his father, James I, ascended the English throne in 1603. The death of his older brother Henry in 1612 made Charles heir to the throne.

Shy and insecure, he suffered from a stammer and lacked the confidence to face criticism. This was compounded by his strong belief in the Divine Right of Kings, which meant that he saw no need to explain his actions to his people since he was answerable only to God, the source of his power as King.

He became King in 1625 and married the French Catholic princess Henrietta Maria. As a result of this and his preference for the elaborate Arminian style of Protestant worship, many feared that he was sympathetic to Catholicism. This, together with his failure to call Parliament for eleven years between 1629 and 1640, and the means by which he governed and raised money during this 'Personal Rule', meant that when he was finally forced to call Parliament in 1640 there was a strong desire among MPs for 'redress of grievances'. Although he made significant concessions, his methods of dealing with Parliament, particularly his failure to explain his actions, meant that some MPs could not accept that he intended to abide by the new restraints on him.

By the autumn of 1642 he was involved in a Civil War, and in 1646 he admitted defeat and surrendered. However, the divisions among his enemies encouraged him to start a second war. He lost, but more seriously the Parliamentary Army now felt that he had gone against God's will in failing to accept defeat, and that he was, therefore, guilty of treason. Consequently the Army seized the political initiative and forced his trial. The only possible verdict was 'guilty'.

Sentence was carried out on 30 January 1649 when Charles was beheaded in front of his palace at Whitehall in London.

Parliament failing to answer the demands of his soldiers – the causes for which they had fought in the Civil Wars – Cromwell at first tried to put their case in Parliament. He made little headway; in April 1653 his patience snapped and he forcibly ejected the MPs, just as they were about to call a general election. Power now lay with the **Army Council**, of which he was the head. When a new assembly to replace Parliament was nominated, Cromwell urged its members to undertake the reforms he had failed to achieve earlier. His particular concern was for 'godly reformation' – encouraging people to live as good, God-fearing Christians.

Army Council: the officers, and representatives of the rank and file soldiers, of Parliament's Army.

Cromwell as Head of State

Within months, however, the new assembly's members fell out. By now Cromwell's army colleague, **John Lambert**, had produced a blueprint for a new style of government, with a Head of State, Council and Parliament. When the assembly handed power back to the Army Council, Cromwell was invited to be Head of State. In December 1653, at the age of 54, he became Lord Protector Cromwell. He did not have absolute power, as the new constitution (known as the Instrument of Government) obliged him to seek the approval of his Council. Although together they could make new laws until a Parliament was called, all laws would then have to be approved by the Parliament. Cromwell and his Council began a vigorous programme of reform of religion and the law in line with the Army's demands.

Rule of the Major-Generals: a system whereby England was divided into areas each under a Major-General who was responsible for the militia and various other aspects of local government.

Problems arose, however, when a Parliament finally met in the autumn of 1654. The members clearly did not share the Protector's vision of godly rule. The tension between Cromwell's dual aims of 'healing and settling' the nation and introducing godly rule ultimately proved incompatible. On this occasion the Parliament was dismissed without passing any legislation. In 1655 a controversial new experiment in local government, the **Rule of the Major-Generals**, was tried. A second Parliament met in 1656–7 and proved more amenable in its first session. Cromwell as well as the MPs compromised, with Cromwell abandoning the unpopular Major-Generals

John Lambert (1619–84)
A gifted parliamentary soldier, Lambert was also involved in composing the Army's constitutional programme. Together with Henry Ireton he drew up the Heads of the Proposals in 1647. In 1653 he wrote the first draft of the Instrument of Government. He served on Cromwell's Council of State, but was dismissed after opposing the offer of the crown to Cromwell in 1657. He was involved in trying to prevent the restoration of monarchy in 1659–60, was tried in 1662 and condemned to death. He was reprieved, but sentenced to life imprisonment.

**Richard Cromwell
(1626–1712)**
Third son of Oliver Cromwell, he served as an MP in 1654 and 1656. He became a member of the Council of State in 1657 and of the new Upper House under the Humble Petition and Advice in 1658. With relatively little political experience he was nominated by his father as his successor shortly before Oliver's death. He abdicated in return for personal protection in April 1659 and fled into exile in 1660. He returned to England in 1680.

experiment. It even seemed that Cromwell was giving serious consideration to the offer of the crown made to him by the MPs in February 1657. In the end, however, he rejected this ultimate accolade. From his speeches and letters it appears that the most important influence on this decision was his appeal to Biblical precedents (providence). He believed that God's will can be discerned through study of the Bible, and his aim was to carry out that will. The ways in which he applied his beliefs throughout his political career form an important theme in any study of Oliver Cromwell.

Under the new constitution, the Humble Petition and Advice, Cromwell remained Lord Protector. After the death of his favourite daughter, Elizabeth, in August 1658, his health declined. He died, on his 'lucky day', 3 September, the anniversary of his victories at Dunbar (1650) and Worcester (1651), of a malarial fever. At his state funeral his effigy was decked in the trappings of a king. He was succeeded as Lord Protector by his eldest surviving son, **Richard**. The Protectorate only survived Oliver by eight months.

Was religion Cromwell's main motivation?

> **What were Cromwell's religious beliefs?**

> **How have historians interpreted Cromwell's actions?**

Framework of events

1644	July: The battle of Marston Moor
	December: the Self-Denying Ordinance is introduced
1645	April: Cromwell's first exemption from the Self-Denying Ordinance
1653	April: Cromwell dissolves the Rump Parliament
	July: the Nominated Assembly is installed
	December: the Nominated Assembly hands power back to Cromwell
	Cromwell becomes Lord Protector
1657	February: Cromwell is offered the crown
	April: Cromwell declines the crown
	May: Humble Petition and Advice is accepted by Cromwell

O NE of the questions historians ask about people in the past is what motivated them. This is particularly pertinent for Oliver Cromwell, a man who lived in relative obscurity for most of his life. He reached the highest position achieved by any English civilian in history, yet he certainly did not anticipate this role when he went to London as an MP in 1640 or even when he began raising a company to fight the King in 1642. In this chapter, the aim is to examine incidents in Cromwell's life that can throw light on his motives, especially ones about which there is disagreement among commentators.

It may seem strange to make religious beliefs the starting point of a study of a political figure. However, most recent historians agree that the key to understanding Cromwell's political actions lies in acknowledging that his religious beliefs were the guiding principle behind them. Hugh Trevor-Roper claims that, 'No political career is so full of undefended inconsistencies as his'. Yet Colin Davis concludes that, 'he may have had to work with "solutions" which remained rough round the edges but the set of aspirations at their heart remained consistent and enduring'.

Why is there disagreement about Cromwell's motives?

Republicans: those who wanted he country to be ruled by a Council and Parliament, without a named Head of State.

There are several reasons for disagreement. Firstly, on a number of occasions Cromwell appeared to let down or betray former allies. He did this to the Levellers in the Spring of 1649 and the **republicans** in 1653. Inevitably these men were suspicious of Cromwell's stated motives, which were usually expressed in religious terms. Leveller leaders wrote in 1649, 'You shall scarce speak to Cromwell about any thing, but he will lay his hand on his breast, elevate his eyes, and call God to record, he will weep, howl, and repent, even while he doth smite [strike] you under the first rib'. Yet many historians, having examined events in great detail, do not find such criticism justified. In *The Cromwellian Protectorate* (2002), Barry Coward asserts that Cromwell was so consistent in attributing events to the will of God that he should be considered sincere.

Providence: the belief that nothing happens by chance, and that God reveals his approval or disapproval of men's actions by rewarding the godly and punishing the sinful.

Secondly, for Cromwell, acting in accordance with his religious beliefs (following divine **providence**) often led to an increase in his power. This does lay his motives open to question. For example, accepting the position of Lord Protector in 1653 as 'Moses leading the children of Israel out of Egypt', gave Cromwell almost unlimited power, at least for a year until his first Protectorate Parliament met. This led contemporaries to accuse Cromwell of hypocrisy or self-seeking ambition. However, the modern historian Ronald Hutton is also sceptical: 'Defenders of Cromwell would suggest that … he was waiting to see which way the will of God was tending and then following it. Perhaps he was, but then God clearly always wanted Cromwell to survive politically.'

Putney Debates: discussions held at Putney Church among members of the Army Council. The debates centred around radical constitutional ideas put forward by the Levellers.

In another example, at the **Putney Debates** in 1647, Cromwell wanted a prayer meeting on the second morning to seek out God's will on constitutional issues. However, in his introduction to the transcript of the debates, the historian A. S. P. Woodhouse suggests that this may in fact have been a delaying tactic. It was in Cromwell's interests that the radical political programme put before the Army Council should not be adopted. And the abrupt end brought to the debates by the escape of Charles I from custody was, according to some contemporaries, engineered by Cromwell. The fact that Charles escaped from the hands of one of Cromwell's relatives and was recaptured by another adds weight to the argument of the conspiracy theorists, but modern historians have acknowledged that there is no hard evidence that Cromwell was involved.

What were Cromwell's religious beliefs?

Non-conformist: a Protestant who does not belong to the Church of England. From 1828, non-conformists were allowed to stand for political office in Britain. They took a positive view of Cromwell because he was in favour of religious toleration.

Oliver Cromwell has sometimes been labelled a Puritan and sometimes an Independent. Nineteenth-century **non-conformist** historians favoured the latter because it fitted better with their own more open and tolerant attitudes. The label 'Puritan' really goes hand-in-hand with references to the seventeenth-century constitutional upheavals as the Puritan Revolution – it is not a label used by Cromwell's contemporaries.

Nineteenth- and early twentieth-century historians tended to use these labels for Cromwell, but the historian Colin Davis now warns against this approach. It is very difficult to categorise people from the 1640s and 1650s from a religious perspective, because their beliefs evolved considerably, and so did the religious groups to which they belonged. It was only after Cromwell had died, and the monarchy had been restored, that the beliefs and practices of these groups became more formalised.

Book of Common Prayer: the official service book of the Church of England. Its use was compulsory in the seventeenth century except between 1644 and 1660.

There is little evidence to help us determine Cromwell's exact religious beliefs. He left no writings on the subject and it is not even clear which form of worship he followed once the **Book of Common Prayer** was no longer compulsory. His letters and speeches do show that he had a thorough knowledge of the Bible. Like many people at the time, he is often labelled as a Puritan, and he studied at the strongly Puritan Sidney Sussex College. Although we cannot be precise about the development of his religious beliefs, we do know that by the time he rose to prominence he had strongly-held views, some of which were unusual for his time.

As a deeply religious man, Cromwell followed policies that he hoped would lead the people of Britain to 'godly reformation'. He talked of a 'reformation of manners', meaning a move towards a sober, God-fearing lifestyle. This does not mean that he never enjoyed himself or thought that others should not, but that he believed entertainment and pastimes should avoid pagan practices (such as maypole dancing), blasphemy (taking God's name in vain), and inappropriate behaviour on the Sabbath (or other holy days

James Nayler (c.1618–60)

A leading early Quaker, who was successful in converting many to the faith but often fell foul of the authorities. In October 1656 he was led into Bristol on a donkey by his followers, in a re-enactment of Christ's entry into Jerusalem. This led to his trial on a charge of blasphemy. The death sentence was not applied when he was found guilty, but he was severely mutilated and imprisoned. The illustration is of Nayler being whipped and having his tongue bored. After his release in 1659 he continued preaching but was set upon by robbers near Huntingdon and killed.

such as Christmas). Put in religious terms, Cromwell believed in following the Ten Commandments.

Cromwell frequently referred to providence (see page 17) when explaining events. Puritans in the mid-seventeenth century believed that the success of a course of action depended on God's approval. They therefore wanted to be sure what God wanted before they took action, and they blamed themselves for misinterpreting the signs if the action was unsuccessful. Bible stories were taken to be the most fruitful source for revealing God's providence or will. The problem with this approach is that interpretation of the Bible is not a straightforward exercise. It is often possible to cite contradictory examples, and this allowed Cromwell's enemies to claim that his interpretation of God's will was wrong – or was being used to promote his own career.

More unusually for his time, Cromwell was tolerant of a range of approaches to worship. However, this does not mean that he believed in total liberty of conscience – rather, that there was more than one route to a godly society and that the end was more important than the means. He only objected to what went directly against the Bible. He also believed that those who were mistakenly over-enthusiastic should be given the opportunity to repent. The case of **James Nayler** presents the clearest evidence of this. Unlike the MPs, Cromwell did not advocate the death penalty to punish Nayler's blasphemy, on the grounds that he was mentally disturbed.

Earl of Manchester Edward Montagu, 2nd Earl of Manchester, (1602–71)		
One of the Puritan members of the Long Parliament, he was charged with high treason by the King in 1642, but escaped arrest. In 1643, he was	appointed Major-General in the army. He fought at Marston Moor and Newbury in 1644 but became increasingly cautious and reluctant to engage the enemy. He resigned his commission in 1645 under the terms of the Self-Denying Ordinance.	Thereafter he sat in the Lords, attempting to negotiate a settlement with the King and opposing his trial and execution. He then retired from public life, but supported the restoration of the monarchy and later held office under Charles II.

How have historians interpreted Cromwell's actions?

In mid-1644 a crisis of leadership struck the Parliamentary Army fighting the King in the first Civil War. After the parliamentary victory at Marston Moor in July, the advantage was not followed up. The second battle of Newbury in late October was indecisive and subsequently the King was allowed to relieve the strategically-important Donnington Castle. Cromwell accused the **Earl of Manchester** of being reluctant to fight the war to a military victory. He was right. Manchester, worried by the religious, political and social upheaval that may result if Parliament won the war, had hesitated.

A closer look at this quarrel demonstrates Cromwell's religious motivation. Until this point, both Manchester and Cromwell had allowed a greater freedom of religious practice within their Army than would have been tolerated amongst civilians. Manchester now seemed to realise the full implications of this once the war was over, and wanted to reach a settlement with the King so that a strong national church could be imposed. From Cromwell's point of view, however, a peace based on the treaty between Parliament and the Scots was unacceptable. It would mean an English church on the **presbyterian** Scottish model. This would deny the freedom of worship that Cromwell advocated. Besides this, Cromwell interpreted the victory at Marston Moor as an indication that God now wanted Parliament to win the war. Failing to follow up the advantage indicated that Manchester was no longer committed to the cause.

Presbyterian: a form of church organisation which put the church in the hands of elected ministers and lay elders rather than appointed bishops.

The Self-Denying Ordinance, 1645

The division also led to conflict between Cromwell and Manchester in Parliament. However, in December 1644, perhaps appreciating that such a quarrel would ultimately undermine the position of both of them, Cromwell proposed that rather than analysing past mistakes, it would be better to seek solutions. These included continuing to remodel the Army as the New Model Army, and passing the law known as the **Self-Denying Ordinance**. It was this law that led to Cromwell being accused of furthering his own interests. As the only MP who retained high-ranking Army office, Cromwell was uniquely placed to rise to political power.

The debate centres around whether, when he put forward the Ordinance, Cromwell could have anticipated that he would be made exempt from it. Certainly, when the Ordinance was introduced, there was no provision at all for exemptions. Early on, Parliament refused to exempt its own commander, the Earl of Essex. If Essex's friends could lose such a vote, Cromwell and his allies could not hope to win. However, once **Sir Thomas Fairfax** had been appointed as the new Parliamentary commander, Cromwell's chances improved significantly, and it was Fairfax who urged Parliament to renew Cromwell's commission. So when Cromwell went to resign his commission in April 1645, he was ordered to carry on campaigning, with his commission renewed for forty days. It was during this period that Cromwell made his decisive contribution at the Battle of Naseby. Although the April vote was a close one, on every successive occasion when Cromwell's commission expired it was renewed.

These short-term appointments meant that Cromwell was under frequent scrutiny, so his contributions in Parliament were restricted. This is noticeable on the occasions on which religious settlement was debated. Cromwell raised the issue of toleration, but did not press his case when the majority clearly opposed him. If ambition was his primary motivation, then he had done himself no service as a politician. It is also debatable whether an ambitious politician would have remained with the Army as long as Cromwell did. After the Battle of Naseby in June 1645, the war amounted to little more than a mopping-up operation. Cromwell's presence with the Army was surely not essential, yet that is where he chose to remain.

It is little surprise that opinion is divided among historians about Cromwell's motives in promoting the Self-Denying Ordnance. Cromwell himself referred in 1653 to the sequence of events as an example of God's intervention on the side of His people. However, since by this time he was in a far more powerful position, and the Self-Denying Ordinance marked the start of his route to power, this can hardly be taken as an objective view. Yet

Self-Denying Ordinance: a law, put forward by Cromwell himself, which stated that no Member of Parliament of either house could hold civil or military office. The law was passed in April 1645. All members with a commission in the Army had to resign it by May 1645. However, Cromwell and a couple of other MPs were made exempt.

Sir Thomas Fairfax (1612–71)
During the early part of the Civil War, Fairfax fought in Yorkshire, where he commanded part of the Parliamentarian Army at Marston Moor. In February 1645 he was appointed Captain-General of the New Model Army, a position he retained until 1650. In that year he resigned rather than invade presbyterian Scotland. He withdrew from public life until 1659, but was then involved in bringing about the restoration of the Stuarts.

many modern historians, like Colin Davis, suggest that Cromwell showed only selfless commitment to the Parliamentary cause by his actions. J. Adamson believes that Cromwell always did plan to ask for exemption, but wanted to avoid being accused of hypocrisy and self-interest – 'it was a risk, but perhaps a calculated one'.

Peter Gaunt is also sceptical of Cromwell's motives. He interprets Cromwell's support of Fairfax as the leader of the New Model Army as an indication that he did plan to remain in both Parliament and the Army, since it was Fairfax who urged that Cromwell be retained in the Army. The evidence is ambiguous, and a case can be argued for either motive: religious conviction or self-seeking ambition. Historians tend to base their opinions on an overall assessment of Cromwell's actions, rather than on the analysis of a single event.

The constitutional changes of 1653

Cromwell's motives are also called into question over the major constitutional changes made in 1653. On 20 April, Cromwell used military force to dissolve the Rump Parliament. Power was now in the hands of the Army and hence its commander – Oliver Cromwell. The Army set about introducing a new government and in July a new assembly met (sometimes called the Barebones, or Little Parliament). The intention was that it would sit until November 1654. However, in mid December a majority of the members handed power back to Cromwell. Under the terms of a new constitution drafted by John Lambert (see page 14), known as the **Instrument of Government**, Cromwell was offered and accepted the title of Lord Protector. Thus he became the country's first, and only, non-royal Head of State.

Instrument of Government: became the constitution of England in late December 1653. Power lay in the hands of a Lord Protector and his Council.

The first question to be asked is, why did Cromwell dissolve the Rump Parliament? Legally, this Parliament could only be dissolved with its own consent. Cromwell's action, using armed soldiers to expel the members, seemed uncomfortably close to that of Charles I. In January 1642 Charles had used soldiers in his attempt to arrest the five members whom he regarded as ring-leaders against him. Cromwell seemed to be over-riding the very parliamentary rights he had fought to defend during the Civil Wars. In May 1653, Cromwell even employed a journalist specifically to deny the claim that in removing the Rump he had denied the liberty of the people of England.

One of the problems in interpreting the event, is that we know it led to Cromwell holding power initially, and within eight months becoming Lord Protector. In other words, he seemed to gain power as a result of his actions. Immediately after the dissolution he had reason to claim that, having been appointed Commander of the Army by Parliament, he was the only legitimate authority in the country. Added to this evidence are the conversations that Bulstrode Whitelocke reported that he had had with Cromwell in 1651 and 1652. In these they allegedly discussed possible future constitutional arrangements, with Cromwell suggesting not only that a mixed or constitutional monarchy might work, but also that a non-royal (himself, perhaps) might become King. Whitelocke's memoirs are widely used as evidence of Cromwell's ambitious intentions, but there is no other evidence to support his account and his memoirs were not published until after Cromwell's death, when Charles II was King and criticising Cromwell was in favour. Whitelocke's memoirs therefore cannot be trusted. However, even if he is a reliable source, the conversation only shows Cromwell considering the implications of possible courses of action. Neither in 1653 nor in 1657 is there any suggestion that Cromwell wanted the crown for the sake of the prestige it would give him.

In asking why Cromwell dissolved the Rump, there are two issues to be considered:

● Why were Cromwell and the Army opposed to the Rump?

● Why did Cromwell act so suddenly and decisively on 20 April?

It is easy to focus too closely on the second question when trying to decide what Cromwell's motives were, but the opposition to the Rump does show clearly the extent to which Cromwell viewed situations in a religious context (and so may well have had an underlying religious motive for his action). By 1653 the Army had a clear sense of being God's instrument in carrying out His will. Not only had they precipitated the trial and execution of the King, but they believed that God had further endorsed their actions by allowing them to triumph over the Irish and then the Scots. The soldiers began to assess the actions of the Rump Parliament and found that they were falling short of the high ideals they had laid out for England, in documents such as the **Heads of Proposals** as well as in the Leveller programme as stated in the **Case of the Army**. Cromwell had a difficult time persuading the soldiers not to intervene in government. He sympathised with their criticism of the Rump, but recognised that the Rump was the legitimate government.

However, by 1653 Cromwell's patience was running thin. The main complaints about the Rump centred on its slowness in bringing

Heads of Proposals: moderate peace proposals drafted by Henry Ireton and submitted to the King by the Army in 1647. These included biennial parliaments and religious toleration.

Case of the Army Truly Stated: a document drafted by John Lilburne reflecting the demands of the Levellers. These included biennial parliaments elected by free-born males over 21 and the redress of social grievances.

Toleration Act: repealed all laws enforcing weekly attendance at church.

Blasphemy Act: outlawed those who claimed to be Christ or whose leader claimed this, along with those who taught that any sin was permissible for the 'saved'.

Adultery Act: made incest and adultery punishable by death, and fornication subject to three months' imprisonment.

about legal reform, social justice, religious toleration and godly reformation. In 1652 and early 1653 Cromwell urged the soldiers to give the Rump more time to introduce acceptable laws. However, faced with demands concerning legal reform, the traditional ruling élite represented in the Rump showed the same reluctance that the Army grandees had done in the Putney Debates. They were afraid that the Army wanted to destroy private property and, to them, land ownership was a fundamental right. The right to social justice was also denied, at least to some former royalists who, unlike the majority, were not pardoned for their actions during the Civil War. The Rump had made some moves towards religious toleration, with the **Toleration Act** of September 1650. However, there was greater emphasis on the suppression of some extreme religious sects. This was demonstrated by the **Blasphemy Act** of April 1650 and the **Adultery Act** of May 1650. Overall, Cromwell became convinced that the Rump, by failing to introduce the Army's programme of reforms, was going against God's will.

The events of April 1653 also centred on the key issue of parliamentary reform. There is no evidence showing what exactly the Rump was planning. One theory is that they were planning a series of by-elections, rather than a general election. This would clearly be undermining the rights of the English people to elect MPs in a general election. Another possibility was that they were going to change the terms of elegibility for election. Without strict control over who was eligible to stand for election, a new House of Commons would reinstate the Stuart monarchy and a national church. It may have seemed to Cromwell that the only way to achieve what he believed God wanted was for the Army to seize power.

On 19 April, Cromwell was under the impression that a meeting of MPs and Army officers had established acceptable terms for a general election. However, on the morning of 20 April, word reached him that the Rump was about to vote on unacceptable terms. It was at this point that he went to Westminster and expelled the Rump. He may have misunderstood the Bill before the Rump or he may simply have wanted to take power. As Cromwell pocketed and later destroyed the only copy of the proposals on which the Rump was about to vote, historians can never know its terms. Cromwell's motives can only be judged against his later statements and actions.

Certainly at this stage Cromwell made no attempt to keep power for himself. After discussions and heated disagreement in the Army Council, a new assembly was established, known as the Nominated Assembly. In July, Cromwell made a long speech to the members. It was full of Biblical references, alluding to the sequence of events by

A contemporary print showing Cromwell dissolving the Rump Parliament.

which God had shown the people of England what His plan was for them. Cromwell clearly had high hopes, yet within months these were dashed. Although significant progress was made by the Assembly, the sticking point, yet again, was the religious settlement. A majority of the members then signed a document handing power back to Cromwell, Commander of the Army.

A second charge levelled at Cromwell in 1653 came from republicans who were critical of the way in which he brought the Commonwealth to an end by accepting the position of Lord Protector. The new constitution bore some resemblance to the old system of King, Privy Council and Parliament which had been dismantled in 1649. Why did Cromwell take on this role, apparently reverting to a more traditional form of government? This seemed to go against God's will, as revealed in 1649, to rid England of a monarchy and approve a commonwealth.

Despite Cromwell's claims that he knew nothing of what was to happen, Barry Coward argues in *The Cromwellian Protectorate* (2002) that Cromwell was well aware of events, and that he welcomed the resignation of the Nominated Assembly and the hand-over of power to him. However, he does also acknowledge that the common characteristic of the key protagonists in establishing the Protectorate was their independent religious views. Becoming Lord

Protector allowed Cromwell to assume political power, suggesting he was ambitious, but it also meant he could introduce the religious toleration he believed in. Once again it is impossible to separate what suited Cromwell's religious aims, from what benefited him in terms of gaining power. Coward's conclusion is that, 'the exercise of political cunning is not incompatible with the pursuit of high ideal: on most occasions when Cromwell acted ruthlessly, he did so primarily to advance his hopes of bringing about a godly reformation in Britain'. A less sympathetic interpretation is still possible, but certainly Cromwell made no attempt to rule arbitrarily. In the 12 September 1654 speech to his first Protectorate Parliament he also spoke of how he welcomed a balanced constitution in which his powers were limited and claimed, "I called not myself to this place". He no doubt sincerely believed what he said.

1657: Cromwell refuses the Crown

The underlying tension between Army and civilian government remained a feature of the Cromwellian Protectorate. This was inevitable given the high level of taxation needed to maintain the Army and was exacerbated by the notorious Rule of the Major-Generals in 1655–57. In February 1657, the Second Protectorate Parliament considered a new constitution to replace Lambert's Instrument of Government. The document in its final format is known as the Humble Petition and Advice. As well as the introduction of a second chamber in Parliament, there were many subtle changes in the balance of power, but a key feature was the reintroduction of monarchy, with the title of King being offered to Oliver Cromwell. The petition was finally accepted by Cromwell except for this last point. On 26 June 1657 he was re-invested as Lord Protector in a far more elaborate ceremony than that of December 1653.

Hostile contemporaries such as the royalist Clarendon and the republican Ludlow both believed that Cromwell was ambitious to be King, and that he had to be persuaded not to accept the title. These commentators, however, are not reliable. Two other commentators, who were present when Cromwell met with some Army officers, both reported that Cromwell said he was indifferent to the title – that it was 'but a feather in a man's cap'. Yet the absence of an objective contemporary account, and the five long weeks of soul-searching, suggest that Cromwell did at least seriously consider accepting the title.

Perhaps the main attraction for Cromwell, and the reason he hesitated for so long, was that taking the title of King might help

An engraving from *The Emblem of England's Distraction*, 1658. Cromwell is dressed in armour and carrying a sword which is passing through the crowns of England, Scotland and Ireland. The words at the top mean 'I worship only God', and many scenes from the Bible are depicted.

Landmark Study   **The articles that changed people's views**

Blair Worden, 'Toleration and the Cromwellian protectorate', (1984) 'Providence and politics in Cromwellian England' (1985) and 'Oliver Cromwell and the sin of Achan' (1985).

Until Blair Worden published his series of articles in the mid-1980s, most historians interpreted Cromwell's religious views using terms and concepts from a period later than the mid-seventeenth century. Blair Worden changed the way that historians interpreted Cromwell's religion because he placed Cromwell's beliefs in the context of mid-seventeenth century Protantism. In particular, he recognised that religious belief was in a state of flux. This meant that many sincere Protestants were 'seeking the truth', that sects were nebulous and the beliefs of individuals changed and developed during the course of their lives. Thus he rejected earlier labels for Cromwell, such as 'Puritan', 'Calvinist', 'Independent' and 'darling of the sects'. He re-appraised Cromwell's religious toleration. He also recognised the centrality of the concept of providence for Cromwell and many of his contemporaries. He used this concept to explain why Cromwell agonised over a range of decisions from the execution of the King onwards, and to explain why Cromwell could consider pursuing apparently contradictory courses of action.

him achieve his two aims – which were virtually mutually exclusive – of 'healing and settling' of the nation, and of a godly reformation. Taking the crown might well reconcile more of the traditional ruling élite to the regime. The introduction of an Upper House in Parliament was also attractive to Cromwell. He and his Council would have the power to nominate its members, and it would act as a check on the Commons. A further point was that there had been no clear mechanism for choosing his own successor. The Humble Petition would allow Cromwell to name his successor. This could be interpreted as ambition on his part, but possibly of greater importance to Cromwell was the need to secure the regime and all it stood for.

On the other hand, Army officers placed tremendous pressure on Cromwell to reject the crown. He had several meetings with them and on 7 March a hundred officers presented him with a petition, urging him to reject the crown. The rank and file, as well as the officers, were still heavily influenced by the concept of 'the cause' for which they had fought, interpreting the abolition of monarchy as the will of God. Certainly the generals were determined that Cromwell should not accept the crown, with three of them threatening to resign if he became King. However, both before and after this point Cromwell did not hesitate to suppress Army dissent, and had no difficulty in doing so. He could, perhaps, have ignored the officers, although hostility to kingship may have been too widespread in the Army to risk accepting the title. Overall, it looks very possible that the Army played a significant role in Cromwell's decision, and the reason Cromwell gave – that it was God's will – did coincide with the arguments put forward by the Army.

The only motive for Cromwell's rejection of the crown that is not plausible is the one put forward by a Venetian Ambassador in March 1657. He suggested that Cromwell would stay as Lord Protector because he would have more power in that role than if he were to become King. Since Cromwell accepted all the other clauses of the Humble Petition and Advice, this reason seems unlikely. He had lived in the royal palace at Hampton Court since the Rump had granted him this honour, together with £4000 a year income, after his victory at Worcester in 1651. As Lord Protector he had to heed the advice of his Council and use Parliament to pass laws.

An unfinished portrait of Cromwell by Samuel Cooper. The fundamental difference in Cromwell's approach compared with that of the Stuarts is indicated by the presence in the portrait of his physical blemishes. A royal portrait would have disguised the warts on his face.

The Council of State's secretary, John Thurloe, reported in early April that Cromwell had definitely decided to accept the crown. The fact that it was subsequently rejected probably indicates that Cromwell's intentions were difficult to discern even for those closest to him, rather than that he changed his mind. Finally, after five weeks of consideration, Cromwell refused the crown. His interpretation of God's will was clear. On 13 April he told the parliamentary committee, 'God has seemed providentially not only to strike at the family [Stuart] but at the name [king].' He continued, referring to the story of Joshua in the Old Testament, 'I will not seek to set up that which providence hath destroyed, and laid in the dust; I would not build Jericho again.' However, as was often the case, Cromwell had achieved what he wanted and could justify it in terms of what God had ordained. He finally rejected the title on 8 May on the grounds that accepting it would go against providence.

Ultimately, interpretations of Cromwell's motives depend on whether or not the historian believes that Cromwell was sincere. His style of speech, with its frequent biblical references, is so alien to the twenty-first century that it is difficult to accept. However, through detailed analysis of Cromwell's letters and speeches, most modern historians have come to the conclusion that, even if he sometimes deceived himself, his beliefs were sincerely held and his motives genuine.

Was religion Cromwell's main motivation?

1. Read the following extract and answer the question.

    'Cromwell referred constantly to the role of 'providences' in pointing towards God's will and the 'necessity' of conforming to it. The thrust of recent scholarship has been to take these statements very seriously as a genuine indication of his inner frame of mind. Most recent writers have inclined towards seeing Cromwell as basically sincere even if there was an element of self-deception that allowed him to put the most favourable possible gloss on his own motives.'

    (David Smith, *Cromwell and the Interregnum*, Blackwell, 2003, p3.)

    Using the information in this chapter, show how far you agree with recent interpretations of Cromwell's motives.

2. Explain why there has been so much disagreement about Cromwell's sincerity.

Was Cromwell radical or conservative?

How radical was Cromwell as an Army leader?

Was Cromwell a radical or a conservative politician?

Did Cromwell want radical constitutional change?

How radical were Cromwell's religious policies during the Protectorate?

	Framework of events
1642	First Civil War begins
1647	July: Heads of Proposals presented to Charles I
	October–November: the Putney Debates
1653	the Instrument of Government
1654	the first Protectorate Parliament meets
1655	the Rule of the Major-Generals (to 1657)
1656	the second Protectorate Parliament meets

What were Cromwell's aims?

When investigating the role that individuals have played, historians try to work out what their aims were. In the case of Cromwell this at first appears to be straightforward. He made clear on many occasions that he wanted greater religious toleration. Since religious toleration can be seen as forward-thinking, and certainly represented a major change in government policy, he can clearly be categorised as a radical.

However, in constitutional and political matters, Cromwell is now generally considered to have been conservative. At least until 1647 he was committed to the idea of monarchy and he remained convinced throughout that Parliament had an important role to play in government. As Lord Protector, he said that he wanted to achieve 'healing and settling' of the nation, which involved compromise with the traditional ruling élite over the constitution. As a result, he worked with institutions that looked remarkably similar to the old

Franchise: the right to vote in an election, especially one in which a parliament is elected.

system of monarch, Council and Parliament. Nor did he want to democratise politics, for example by extending the **franchise**.

Why is there disagreement about Cromwell's aims?

When considering how radical or conservative he was, Cromwell can appear contradictory. He appointed men to his regiments during the Civil War regardless of their social position, but insisted that only property owners should have a political role. He worked with the Levellers in the Army, but turned against them after the execution of the King. He argued for the execution of the King, but considered taking the crown himself. As Blair Worden says in *The Rump Parliament 1648–1653* (1974), 'It would be hard to exaggerate the influence of the ambiguities of Cromwell's political temperament on Rump politics. A conservative by social instinct and early political training, he was inspired to spiritual radicalism by his role as God's instrument of victory in the Civil War, by his intimacy with his troops, and by his informal but weighty responsibilities as patron of the religious sects. What resulted was (to simplify) a kind of ideological schizophrenia.' Colin Davis, however, warns against regarding the apparent paradoxes of Cromwell's career as an explanation for his actions. 'The contradictoriness of the paradox,' he warns, 'while it may illuminate the problem, never explains or resolves it.'

Henry Ireton (1611–1651)
From a Puritan gentry family, he was involved in the Civil Wars from the outset, and his fortunes were closely linked to those of Oliver Cromwell. He was also heavily involved in the constitutional debates between the Civil Wars. A clearer political thinker than Cromwell and also more conservative, he exerted a strong influence on him. He was the author of the Army's proposals for a settlement with the King, called the Heads of Proposals. At the Putney Debates, he argued forcefully against extending the franchise. He was instrumental in engineering the purge of Parliament in December 1648, having become disillusioned with the King. In 1646 he married Cromwell's daughter, Bridget. He went with Cromwell to Ireland in 1649, remaining there when Cromwell returned to England. He died there, of a fever, in 1651.

Another factor to consider is that neither the 'radical' nor the 'conservative' labels are as accurate as they initially appear. It is necessary to look more carefully at the evidence of what Cromwell intended. The interpretations of contemporaries cannot be accepted uncritically. All had their own agenda. When previous allies of Cromwell felt let down, they accused him of betraying their cause, and this was often on the grounds that he had become conservative. In the Leveller pamphlet, *England's New Chains Discovered*, published in February 1649, the charge of hypocrisy is clearly levelled at Cromwell and **Ireton**, the Army leaders. They were accused of manipulating both Army and Parliament, particularly since the natural rights of the freeborn Englishman demanded by the Army were being undermined by this time.

Those who were Cromwell's enemies from the start, on the other hand, might emphasise his radicalism, as it was this aspect of his policies that they feared. For example, one of his opponents during the Civil War complained that he chose common men to be officers, while dismissing 'honest gentlemen'.

More commonly among contemporaries, however, it was Cromwell's methods that were criticised. He was seen as dictatorial and **tyrannical**. At times he grew so frustrated with Parliament that he dismissed it. (This happened in 1653 to the Rump and in 1655 to his first Protectorate Parliament.) It seems that Cromwell would and could only work with a Parliament that reflected his views. Later, after royalist uprisings, he imposed the Rule of the Major-Generals. Although it is generally accepted that his primary purpose was religious – to impose godly rule – rather than military, the charge that he was a military dictator has frequently been made. Certainly his regime was unpopular with many people. Besides this, his treatment of those who challenged the legality of his government, for example by refusing to pay taxes, can also be seen as tyrannical.

Tyrannical: ruling cruelly or unfairly

It is also important to consider the changing context in which Cromwell operated – moving from Civil War and regicide in the 1640s to the attempt to re-establish effective government in the 1650s. To expect a man to appear consistent throughout is, perhaps, to ask the impossible. Blair Worden called Cromwell's vacillation between social conservatism and spiritual radicalism 'a kind of ideological schizophrenia'. Colin Davis, in contrast, claims that, 'It is possible to develop a case for some consistency in Cromwell's political career in the pursuit of civil and religious liberty within a governmental framework which would be acceptable to most of his compatriots'.

How radical was Cromwell as an Army leader?

Cromwell became a soldier in the summer of 1642. Along with about fifty-five fellow MPs, he took an active role fighting in the Civil War. Like many of the others, he was relatively old (43) to be embarking on such a career. Unlike most of the other MPs, he became a very successful tactician, and, more importantly, survived the introduction of the Self-Denying Ordinance (see page 21). However, it is not his military skill so much as the way in which he picked and promoted his officers and the extent of his religious toleration within the ranks, which singles him out as radical as an Army officer.

When war between King and Parliament seemed inevitable, he returned to his home area and, with the rank of captain, began to raise a troop of cavalry soldiers. In September 1642, he and the sixty men under his command were called on to join the main Parliamentary Army under the Earl of Essex. He was probably present at the indecisive Battle of Edgehill in October 1642, and seeing the action confirmed to him the need for a better trained and organised force than Parliament currently fielded. By early 1643 he had been ordered to raise a regiment of cavalry and was promoted to the rank of colonel. His double regiment of 'Ironsides', composed of fourteen troops, gained a formidable reputation as soldiers.

How did Cromwell choose his officers?

In conversation with fellow MP John Hampden, he discussed the difficulty in creating a force to match the King's. As was the custom at the time, the King's officers were drawn exclusively from the gentry class. While many gentry did fight for Parliament, Cromwell suggested that Parliament's solution lay in choosing men who were first and foremost convinced of the cause for which they fought. By September 1643, he was describing his men in terms of their religious zeal.

Hence, from the start of his career as a soldier, Cromwell acquired a radical reputation. He famously said, 'I had rather have a plain russet-coated captain that knows what he fights for and loves what he knows than what you call a gentleman and is nothing else'. However, his explanation was practical rather than ideological: 'If you choose godly honest men to be captains of horse, honest men will follow them.' Some contemporaries criticised him for this apparently radical approach. One wrote, 'Colonel Cromwell chooses for his officers not such as were soldiers or men of estate, but such as were common men, poor and of mean [lower class] parentage …' During Cromwell's quarrel with the Earl of Manchester in 1644, the Earl told the House of Lords, '… for his expressions were sometimes against the nobility, that he hoped to live to see never a nobleman in England …'

In the context of the mid-seventeenth century, Cromwell's was an unusual approach. He wanted soldiers who believed in the cause for which they were fighting. In a civil war this might seem essential, yet the war had begun over quarrels in Parliament. Until the Long Parliament met, ordinary people had not been directly involved in political debate. **John Pym** changed this when he stirred up the London mob over the signing of the death warrant of the Earl of Strafford, (Charles I's chief adviser) and the publication of the Grand Remonstrance (a document setting out Parliament's achievements and aims) in 1641. In previous civil wars, such as the Wars of the Roses in the

**John Pym
(1584–1643)**
Pym was an MP in every Parliament from 1621. He was a leading member of the anti-monarchy circle in the Commons in the Long Parliament. Although he was offered the position of Chancellor of the Exchequer in 1641, he was generally a vociferous opponent of the King, and played a leading role in the trial of Strafford. He was responsible for encouraging the publication of the Grand Remonstrance. He was one of the five members whom Charles I attempted to arrest on a charge of treason in January 1642. He was instrumental in creating Parliament's alliance with the Scots in 1643. He died in December 1643 of an internal abscess.

The Battle of Naseby, the first major engagement of the New Model Army. Charles underestimated the Army's strength and attacked against advice. Cromwell's cavalry played a decisive role in the victory.

New Model Army: the Parliamentary Army established in 1645. Before this Parliament had grouped county militias into two associations, the Eastern Association and the Midland Association. However, some men had been reluctant to fight away from their native areas, so to counter this a national army was created.

late fifteenth century, ordinary men had fought for nobles to whom they owed allegiance. By the seventeenth century nobles no longer kept armies of retainers and soldiers fought in exchange for pay. It was Cromwell's belief that it would take more than money to encourage men to kill their fellow countrymen. The **New Model Army**, created in 1645, did not consider itself to be an army of mere mercenaries. Instead, the soldiers regarded themselves as a body whose mission was 'the defence of our own and the people's just rights and liberties'.

However, an examination of the men promoted by Cromwell does not reveal an exclusively lower class body of officers. Many of Cromwell's early appointments were, not surprisingly, from his own family, and hence counted as gentlemen. These included his son, Oliver, and his cousin Edward Whalley. Others were from more ordinary backgrounds, but it is clear that Cromwell had chosen competent soldiers, since four of his early appointments later achieved the rank of general.

Were Cromwell's soldiers religious radicals?

Cromwell allowed a wide range of religious beliefs within the Army. This was radical in two senses: firstly, toleration of a range of views was itself revolutionary; secondly, his men developed into a force that fought for a cause. He allowed his men to worship, pray and even preach if they were moved to do so, although normal practice only permitted preaching under licence. Unfortunately the enthusiasm of

Religious belief in the mid-seventeenth century

The mid-seventeenth century was a period during which Protestant beliefs in England were becoming far more diverse.

At the beginning of the century, the main groupings within English Protestantism were incorporated within the Church of England. This was the established Protestant religion of the country. Legally, all had to attend this Church. The structure of the Church was based on that of the Catholic Church, with a hierarchy appointed from the top. The Head of the Church was the monarch. Until about 1625 the Church was broad, that is, it encompassed people with a range of Protestant beliefs, with Puritans at one extreme and Arminians at the other.

Protestant extremes

Puritans emphasised teaching the people through sermons, so that their beliefs were clearly understood, their knowledge of the Bible was thorough and they would live a simple and God-fearing life. They believed that God had predestined some people to be saved (the elect) and others to be damned (go to hell when they died). Some believed that the structure of the Church of England was too close to that of the Catholic Church and that the Church of England should be further reformed, making it more Protestant. They were the Presbyterians.

Arminians emphasised ritual within services, believing that God should be glorified through beautiful churches and elaborate ceremony. They thought that man had free will to choose whether to believe in God and hence be saved, or not. Under Charles I, this branch of the Church of England was favoured, forcing some people to separate from the Church.

The state church and the development of sects

The conservative view of the ruling élite held that adherence to a state church was necessary for the stability of the country.

However, the upheavals of the 1640s led to disagreements within Parliament about the form of the state church, and weaker enforcement of the law once the Court of High Commission was abolished in 1641 and the Civil Wars began in 1642.

Many Puritans found the doctrine of predestination depressing, since man had no control over his fate. Groups of 'Seekers of the Truth' developed around the country. Those who separated from the state church in this way were the religious radicals of the period, rejecting state control and sometimes even the authority of the Bible.

The experiments of separatists reached a peak around the time of the King's execution in 1649. Besides well-established groups such as Baptists and Independents (now called Congregationalists), there were other more nebulous sects. Not only did some experiment with strange practices and develop extreme beliefs, but the sense of dislocation created an atmosphere in which people could be persuaded that all manner of deviance existed.

From the groups of Seekers, some new sects became established. Fifth Monarchists believed that the political disruption in England indicated the imminent reign of King Jesus. Quakers rejected the imposed discipline of the Church and followed instead the inner guidance of the Holy Spirit. These developments frightened many of the traditional ruling élite because such groups would not adhere to the social and legal conventions that enabled the élite to control the populace. This explains the conservative MPs' attempts in the 1650s to clamp down on such radical sects.

On the whole, radical religious sects were intolerant of one another. However, Oliver Cromwell's radicalism in relation to seventeenth-century norms lay in his willingness to tolerate a range of paths to the final goal of a godly society.

John Lilburne (1614–1657)
Lilburne was a confrontational character who consistently pursued what he regarded as his rights as a freeborn Englishman. These included, so he claimed, the right to freedom of religion. As a Leveller, he promoted the idea of broadening the franchise, but continued to push for equality and fairness of the law. This extended to challenging the trial of the King on the grounds of its illegality and challenging the right of the Rump Parliament to decide on the government of the country after the execution of the King. Consequently he was put on trial, but was acquitted. He ended his days in prison, not because he had broken the law but because he had returned to England after banishment without trial.

some gained them a bad reputation. One troop baptised a horse in urine! Most, however, were godly, sober men. His religious policy, together with the regular pay he obtained for his soldiers, enabled Cromwell to create a disciplined fighting force.

Cromwell was not unique in displaying this level of toleration. The Earl of Manchester, when he was promoted to Major-General of the Eastern Association in 1643, allowed a wide range of religious beliefs among his men. Among Manchester's officers was the future Leveller leader **John Lilburne**. Manchester's toleration, though, was soon abandoned.

In late 1643, Parliament's alliance with the Scots included a commitment to introduce the Scottish, national (Presbyterian) religion into England. The degree of toleration allowed by Cromwell therefore presented problems to his superiors, as he was too radical for them. They attempted to purge his troop of its sectarian officers. The tension continued, as the quarrel between Cromwell and Manchester developed (see page 20). By the end of the War, Cromwell claimed that pursuing a godly reformation was essential in defeating the enemy within. 'Religion [i.e. religious liberty] was not the thing at first contested for' but 'God brought it to that issue at last.' This confirmed the extent to which he was radical. His view reflected that of many in the Army. It would make agreement amongst Parliamentarians on peace terms to present to the King virtually impossible.

Did Cromwell want radical constitutional change?

The first point to note about Cromwell's constitutional ideas is that he showed no signs of having read any of the contemporary books on the subject. In 'Oliver Cromwell and English Political Thought', Johann Sommerville observes that, 'Oliver Cromwell was a man of action and not a deep philosopher'. His thoughts,

Political and constitutional ideas in the mid-seventeenth century

The most widely accepted concept of an ideal government was referred to as the Ancient Constitution. This was backward looking in that it relied on a mythical ideal existing before the Norman Conquest of 1066. It consisted of a monarch, who held power with the consent of the people. This consent was demonstrated and confirmed through the body representing all the people of England, that is, Parliament. However, the MPs were elected only by the landowners, because only those with a stake in the country could have the country's best interests at heart. This political idea depended on the concept of a social hierarchy in which some participated in government, while others were represented.

In constitutions such as the Instrument of Government and the Humble Petition and Advice, the fundamentals of this system of limited monarchy pertained. There was a single Head of State, advised by his Council and a representative Parliament which had to meet regularly, and, by early seventeenth-century standards, frequently.

The Divine Right of Kings

Besides this idea, there was the Divine Right of Kings. Charles I believed his power came from God, not the people, and that he was answerable only to God. This accounts for his reluctance to explain his actions. The Civil Wars were fought largely to establish that English kings were subject to the laws of the people enacted in Parliament, and were answerable to the people through Parliament.

The development of radical ideas

During the 1640s, radical political ideas were easier to print, and also became more widespread as a result of the constitutional upheavals taking place. Based on both Biblical ideas and classical history, the idea of popular sovereignty was adopted by some. They believed that power lay with all the people, who had rights as freeborn Englishmen. Monarchy was inevitably tyrannical, and all power tended to corrupt. Hence there should be annual elections so that MPs would be answerable to the electorate. Some went so far as to assert that all men should vote in elections. The distinction between active and passive citizens, based on land ownership, was abandoned. Levellers were at the forefront in promoting these radical views.

Equality before the law was fundamental to these beliefs. In the eyes of ordinary seventeenth-century men, this depended on low cost, straightforward laws and the use of the English language in the law courts.

Sommerville suggests, were neither subtle nor sophisticated. On the other hand, Colin Davis interprets Cromwell's political actions as increasingly skilled. 'Cromwell's practice of politics, and his thinking about it, began to acquire a degree of sophistication and awareness of difficulties which made him increasingly suspect in the eyes of more zealous, and sometimes more naïve, compatriots. This in turn fuelled a reputation for political manipulation and sophistry [using clever but false arguments].' Cromwell was a practical politician.

Cromwell had limited political experience before the late 1640s. No wonder, then, that his approach matured. Perhaps this goes some way towards explaining the apparent changes in his opinions as circumstances developed. Equally, his religious views must not be forgotten, since they frequently informed his constitutional decisions.

The debate after the First Civil War

In July 1647, Cromwell put the Army's proposals for a settlement to Charles I. These were contained in a document known as the Heads of Proposals and were more moderate than those presented to the King by Parliament. Colin Davis argues that for the remainder of his career Cromwell consistently upheld the fundamental points contained in this document, which comprised a government consisting of a Head of State and Parliament, and religious toleration for Protestants.

In the Putney Debates of November 1647 (see page 17), Cromwell listened critically to the egalitarian ideas of the Leveller-influenced **Agitators**, and showed sympathy for the traditionalist argument against universal manhood suffrage. He believed that simply living under a government was insufficient justification for allowing a man to vote. Like his peers (i.e. the gentry/ruling élite), he accepted that a man needed to have the vested interest of owning land in order to qualify to vote. However, Cromwell tempered his criticism of the Leveller views by stating that he was not completely committed ('wedded and glued', as he put it) to any particular form of government.

Agitators: elected representatives of the regiments. They were members of the Army Council.

What was Cromwell's aim in these debates? Colin Davis suggests that his concern was 'to find political solutions which would embrace as many elements of the political nation as was reasonably possible'. Cromwell believed that the Heads of Proposals offered the best solution, and ultimately argued against the more radical programme in **'The Agreement of the People'**.

'The Agreement of the People': a set of constitutional ideas drawn up by the Agitators and Levellers in October 1647 and debated at Putney.

The Heads of Proposals included:

- Biennial parliaments to sit for 120–240 days
- Parliament to nominate the Officers of State for 10 years
- Parliament to control the militia for 10 years
- Religious toleration for Protestants, with no compulsory national church
- Anti-Catholic legislation

The Agreement of the People included:

- Biennial parliaments, of one chamber
- A redistribution of the seats according to the size of the electorate
- Parliament's powers to be limited: the people would decide on religion and conscription
- No mention of Lords or monarchy

Most historians agree on Cromwell's aims, although they differ regarding the degree of political skill he displayed in the debates. In *Oliver Cromwell* (1991), Barry Coward describes Cromwell as an able mediator, showing flexibility in acknowledging that the franchise might be extended. He does show, however, that when this approach failed, Cromwell had to act more decisively in bringing the debates to a close. In Peter Gaunt's *Oliver Cromwell* (1996), a picture emerges of a less effective Cromwell, making 'limp interventions' in the debate. Gaunt claims that Cromwell was sidelined in a debate that ultimately swung in favour of an extended franchise.

But what of Cromwell's opinions? Davis asserts that in the debates Cromwell came as close as he ever did to revealing the philosophical basis of his constitutional ideas. Cromwell reminded the Army Council that the Army was the servant of Parliament and could not legitimately take action to change the constitution. Secondly, he urged the members of the Council to consider God's will for the nation. This was potentially problematic, as has been seen in Chapter 1, and Cromwell urged the soldiers to be careful when trying to ascertain what God wanted. Nevertheless, Davis claims that Cromwell made significant concessions, accepting that God might want to dismantle the Ancient Constitution (see page 38). Clearly Cromwell did appear at first to make concessions regarding the franchise, but was unable to accept the extreme views supported by the Army Council.

In the debate in Parliament in 1647 about how to proceed when the King had rejected both Parliamentary and Army proposals for a settlement, Henry Marten accused Cromwell of being 'king-ridden' because he seemed unable to contemplate a settlement that did not include a monarch. However, in January 1648 Cromwell apparently wavered. He stated in Parliament, 'We declared our intentions [to preserve] monarchy, and they still are so, unless **necessity** enforce an alteration'. Again, Cromwell had been influenced by his experiences – his failed negotiations with the King – and by the action of the King in simultaneously negotiating for an alliance with the Scots in late 1647.

Necessity: the concept of a God-driven imperative.

The Cromwellian Protectorate

Six years later, in 1654, Cromwell was telling his first Protectorate Parliament, 'The Government by a Single Person and a Parliament is fundamental.' In 1657, while rejecting the offer of the crown, he told his second Protectorate Parliament, 'I am a man standing in the place I am in; which place I undertook not so much out of the hope of doing any good, as out of a desire to prevent mischief and evil ... I am ready to serve not as a King but as a constable if you like.' By this time Cromwell had recognised that it would be impossible to achieve his religious goals without the co-operation of the traditional ruling élite, and his public statements reflected this. He did not, however, abandon the causes he believed in.

Cromwell, it seems, was conservative in his constitutional ideas, though in practice he did not find it easy to work with Parliaments. Nevertheless, historians now generally recognise what some contemporaries found harder to see – that time and again Cromwell returned to the idea that he must try to rule with a representative Parliament.

Was Cromwell a radical or a conservative politician?

How difficult did Cromwell find it to work with Parliament?

In Chapter 1, the reasons for Cromwell's forcible dissolution of the Rump in 1653 were examined. The next time that he met with a Parliament was in September 1654, nearly ten months after he had taken the title of Lord Protector. The new constitution, the

Instrument of Government, stated that:

● a Parliament should meet every three years for a period of at least five months

● until the first Parliament met, Cromwell, with the approval of his Council, was allowed to rule by ordinance, although retrospective consent for new laws would have to be obtained from Parliament

● all those with property worth more than £200 could vote, with the exception of royalists

● those who had fought against Parliament were disabled from sitting in the first four Parliaments unless they had declared their loyalty to the Commonwealth

● the Council had the power to approve the elected members.

In *England in Conflict 1603–1660* (1999), Derek Hirst suggests that Cromwell was uneasy about calling Parliament. Nonetheless, in his opening speech Cromwell was positive in his expectations of what the first Protectorate Parliament could achieve: 'I have not spoken these things as one who assumes dominion over you, but as one that doth resolve to be a fellow servant with you to the interest of the people of these nations', he told the MPs. But there were problems from the outset. Members were not supposed to challenge the fundamentals of the Instrument, yet immediately discussion arose about its religious clauses. These stated that:

● England was to be a Christian country and provision should be made for instructing the population accordingly

● no-one was allowed to force another person to follow a particular form of worship

● freedom of worship was allowed, providing it did not cause harm to others

● any law which contravened these provisions was null and void.

These provisions were considered too radical by the majority of MPs. Even when the Council had purged the Parliament of all those who refused to accept the Instrument, debate continued. Finally, after five lunar months (which are shorter than calendar months), Cromwell dissolved Parliament. It had passed no legislation. Technically Cromwell was not in breach of the constitution, but he was close.

The Common wealth ruleing with a fancing Army

Laws Cuftoms

Statutes Episcopy Monarche

Magna Church Land & tyb
Charta.
prerogative
priviledges nobility
Liberties. & House
of peers.

gaine

Food for a Com
=mon wealth.

The Fruits of a Common wealth.

Anti-Commonwealth satire. The Commonwealth is represented as a dragon, with the ordinary people in chains. They have had their rights destroyed.

Nevertheless, the historian David Smith is clear that, 'Cromwell remained committed to the principle of Parliaments and to the belief that they could serve as an instrument to promote a godly commonwealth. Yet in practice he could never find a Parliament that fulfilled his expectations. The crux of the problem was that he was trying to use an institution designed as the 'representative of the realm' to further a godly agenda that commanded the enthusiastic support of only a minority.' Similarly, Peter Gaunt writes, 'During the 1650s, with a standing army of nearly 60,000 at his command, Cromwell might have been able to dispense with Parliaments and rule by the sword and military edict, at least for a time. In reality he attempted no such thing and, as far as we know, never even toyed with the idea. Even when Parliament after Parliament went astray, his faith in the institution apparently survived unshaken.'

The second Protectorate Parliament also presented Cromwell with problems. Not only did the MPs present him with the Humble Petition and Advice (see page 26), they also angered him by discussing the case of James Nayler over a six-week period (see page 19). Under the Instrument of Government, Parliament had no right to act as a court. This incident was one of the reasons that Cromwell began to accept the need for an 'Upper House' of Parliament to check the powers of the Commons. This made the Humble Petition more attractive to him – because it met a need that had become apparent.

It was more difficult for contemporary Parliamentarians to reconcile themselves to Cromwell's actions. Commonwealthsmen had found it impossible to accept Lord Protector Cromwell. The experiment he tried between his two Protectorate Parliaments was to prove even more controversial.

The Rule of the Major-Generals

In 1655, Cromwell divided the country into ten (later eleven) areas and placed each under the control of an Army Major-General. Was this military rule? Was it dictatorship? If it was either of these, then this was a very radical move indeed, because martial law was unprecedented in England.

By early 1655, the legitimacy of Cromwell's regime was being challenged. Royalist uprisings over the Christmas period in 1654 had not been serious, but in the spring, Penruddock's rising in the south-west had more followers. Besides this there were high-profile, if relatively isolated, legal challenges, such as the acquittal of the London merchant George Cony after he had refused to pay a fine for non-payment of customs duties. The first Parliament had failed to confirm the Instrument of Government, which could therefore be regarded as a military imposition since it was brought in by the Army. Also, if the regime was not legitimate, then it had no right to collect taxes. This was reminiscent of Charles I's problems in the 1620s and 1630s.

In the 1930s and 1940s, historians' interest in the Communist and Fascist dictatorships of Stalin, Mussolini and Hitler led them to draw parallels with Cromwell. However, even those historians who are most critical of Cromwell now, acknowledge that he was no

Landmark Study   **An essay that changed people's views**

Hugh Trevor-Roper, 'Oliver Cromwell and his Parliaments'
(1956). This essay has since been revised, most recently in 1984.

After the Restoration, Cromwell generally had a poor press. He was portrayed as a regicide and punished accordingly by being exhumed and beheaded. From a political point of view he was shown to be a tyrant, ruling illegally and dictatorially. Most importantly, he was regarded as the enemy of Parliament because he looked on Parliament as at best a distraction and at worst a rival. By the 1890s this view was so widely

held that MPs insisted the statue of Cromwell was placed outside the Palace of Westminster rather than within the building. In 1903 S.R. Gardiner's *History of the Commonwealth and Protectorate, 1649–56* went some way in championing Cromwell, but since Trevor-Roper's essay appeared, modern scholarly approaches have been applied. Although historians, including Trevor-Roper, continue to be critical

of Cromwell's manipulation of Parliament, at least this is now based on detailed examination of the proceedings rather than on prejudice. Cromwell may be seen as threatening parliamentary sovereignty more than Charles I did, or as an incompetent parliamentary manager, but there is now no doubt that he always intended that a representative institution should form part of the constitution.

military dictator. The Major-Generals worked with civilians in the localities and there was little use of any of the hallmarks of martial law such as military courts.

The main aim of the Major-Generals was to impose godly reformation. Initially they were mainly occupied with the new tax, the **decimation tax**, which was to fund the new militia. There was a desperate need to reduce the cost of government, and changes in the organisation of the military were a necessary part of this. In terms of godly reformation, the Major-Generals had mixed success. In some areas they co-ordinated effectively with local Puritans. In one area of Lancashire, Major-General Charles Worsley succeeded in closing 215 alehouses. Largely, however, they were unsuccessful, reflecting the limited appeal of a puritanical lifestyle. The system was resented more for its kill-joy policies and the lower class origins of some Major-Generals than its military roots.

Decimation tax: a tax of one-tenth of the estates of known royalists worth over £100 p.a. in lands and £1,500 p.a. in goods.

Cromwell's statue outside the Houses of Parliament (unlike those of the monarchs of England, which are inside). The statue dates from the 1890s.

Finally, Cromwell made no effort to sustain the experiment when his second Protectorate Parliament refused to ratify the decimation tax. Without this tax the system could not be funded. In May 1656, the Major-Generals had been recalled to London and the system was in decline. It had been a desperate response to the events of early 1655. Uprisings against the regime, and perhaps more seriously the failure of the Western design (an expedition to capture Hispaniola from the Spanish), had indicated to Cromwell that God's approval was lacking. The solution in his eyes was to move more swiftly to godly reformation. Without the support of the traditional ruling élite this could not succeed, so Cromwell abandoned the system.

How radical were Cromwell's religious policies during the Protectorate?

What were Cromwell's policies?

By contemporary standards, Cromwell was tolerant. This in itself was radical, but how much religious diversity did he allow? The Instrument of Government embodied the principle of toleration, and Cromwell asked the MPs of his first Parliament, 'Is not liberty of conscience in religion a fundamental?' He also claimed that the first of God's two greatest concerns were to give everyone due and just liberty in religion. During his Protectorate the readmission of the Jews to England was discussed at length in the Council and, although it was never officially sanctioned, Cromwell advocated the measure and Jews were tolerated. Roman Catholics were not, but penal laws against them were not harshly or even systematically applied. In the climate of the mid-seventeenth century, anti-Catholicism is hardly surprising. Freedom of worship for Catholics was not allowed in England until 1778, and even then the laws were greeted with violent riots in London.

The Cromwellian policies focused on creating a godly body of ministers. Two committees were established in 1654. In March, the Committee of Triers was set up to assess the fitness of new candidates to the ministry. The Committee represented a range of religious views, and it tested the learnedness and moral qualities of ministers rather than demanding doctrinal conformity. Similarly, the Committee of Ejectors of August 1654 expelled those who were unfit on the same grounds. Another policy aimed at providing learned and sober ministers involved trying to ensure that the clergy were adequately paid.

Were these policies radical?

These measures were confirmed by the first Protectorate Parliament. The MPs showed a strong desire to regulate religion, providing for and maintaining the ministry and preventing religious 'errors'. Many of them were Presbyterian and they emphasised public conformity to a national ministry. Liberty of conscience was relatively low on their agenda, especially where 'errors, heresies and blasphemies' threatened public order. Such was their concern that the MPs stated that the laws they proposed on these matters should stand even if Cromwell did not agree. It is difficult to know whether Cromwell's displeasure at this was directed towards the content of the laws or the undermining of his power that this represented. Certainly he would not have agreed to the MPs' measures.

Two court cases demonstrate that Cromwell was indeed liberal in comparison with others in authority. The first concerns John Biddle, who had been in conflict with the authorities since 1647, when he published a book denying the divinity of the Holy Spirit. The book was condemned, and burned as blasphemous by the public hangman. The following year Parliament voted for the death penalty for all who denied the Trinity. Biddle wrote against this. By the mid-1650s he was in trouble again for publishing his views, and was exiled to the Isles of Scilly. This was a comparatively light punishment. He was now beyond the scope of the law, and Cromwell gave him ten shillings a week for his needs.

The second case involved the Quaker James Nayler, who was another persistent offender for blasphemy. In 1656 he fell foul of the authorities when he entered Bristol on a donkey, in imitation of Christ's entry into Jerusalem. He was probably mentally unbalanced at the time and there were many petitions for leniency. Nevertheless, Parliament debated the case for days and, despite having no constitutional power to do so, passed a savage sentence on him. This was carried out in full. Cromwell's role in this was to make the sentence less than it might have been. Many members wanted to apply the death penalty, but Cromwell, while disapproving of Nayler's blasphemy, urged leniency.

Compared with his MPs, Cromwell appears radical. In the eyes of the Army, however, he was not radical enough. In 1654 he was petitioned that 'liberty of conscience be allowed, but not to papistry [Catholicism] in publicke worshipp'. The prevalence of Independents and sectaries in the army had made the Leveller policy of liberty of conscience popular, although few of the sects were genuinely tolerant. Rather, they wanted toleration for themselves, but had to accept toleration for all in order to achieve this.

Nevertheless, not even Cromwell wanted religious diversity for its own sake. He simply saw it as a means to an end. Liberty of conscience was permitted because Cromwell believed there is more than one route to godliness. Compared with the intolerance of most sects at the time, this was radical.

Cromwell's policies had an underlying aim, to bring about a 'reformation of manners'. This was not a new idea, and in that sense not radical. Ever since the Elizabethan Church Settlement of 1559, which established the Church of England, some Protestants had viewed the reformation of religion as incomplete. The Catholic-style Church hierarchy had now been dismantled (archbishops and bishops had been deprived of their political role in 1642 and the offices abolished altogether in 1646). In the eyes of the godly, God had shown his approval of this and the execution of the King. However, the people in general were still not living in the style that God required. Hence the campaign against all manner of ungodly behaviour – drunkenness, adultery, fornication, swearing and so on. If Cromwell had been successful he would have brought about deep-seated, radical changes in the way people lived. He was not. The most whole-hearted rejection can be seen in the fate of the experiment with the Major-Generals.

As seen in Chapter 1, Cromwell's religious views have caused controversy largely because they have been misunderstood. He has been variously described as a Puritan and as the champion of the sects. He was more than this, and this is what makes him radical. After the Interregnum religion and politics were less intertwined, although this does not mean that men were indifferent to religious matters. By 1689 non-conformist sects were so well established that it was clearly no longer possible, and many thought it was not even desirable, to insist on attendance at the Church of England. In many ways the policies of the Cromwellian Interregnum foreshadowed the Toleration Act of 1689.

Was Cromwell radical or conservative?

1. Read the following extract and answer the question.

> *'A vigorous warrior in the cause of God and His chosen people, Cromwell's political instincts were to seek moderate solutions to the civil problems of rule. A monarch [Charles I] who abused trust helped to engender a revolutionary situation in which moderate men could only struggle to make an ordered and stable society out of the wreckage. This was Cromwell's tragedy. His greatness is that he did so much more than cling on to the debris. By 1657 he had gone a long way towards finding a stable civilian basis for the regime. But time was running out and the settlement was never to be consolidated. It was a settlement far less radical than those who have aspired to an English Revolution would have wished. But it was admirable none the less.'*

> (J. C. Davis, *Oliver Cromwell*, Arnold, 2001, p201)

   Using the information in this chapter, consider how far you agree that Cromwell's instincts were to seek moderate solutions.

2. How far was Cromwell a political and religious radical?

3 Why is Cromwell seen as both a hero and a villain?

What was Cromwell's role in the execution of Charles I?

What was Cromwell's role in the Irish campaign of 1649?

Did Cromwell betray the English Revolution?

Framework of events

1646	April: Charles I surrenders to the Scots
	June: the end of the First Civil War
	July: Parliament offers Charles peace proposals
1647	June: Army Council set up
	July: Heads of Proposals offered to King
	October–November: Putney Debates
	December: Charles's engagement with the Scots
1648	April–September: Second Civil War
	December: Pride's Purge
1649	January: trial and execution of Charles I
	August: Cromwell arrives in Ireland
	September: siege of Drogheda ends
	October: siege of Wexford ends

Why has there been such strong disagreement about Cromwell?

Cromwell is controversial because he was at the centre of an unprecedented series of events. This means that not only did people at the time – and historians since – find him fascinating, but also that his contemporaries could not view him dispassionately. His actions in the late 1640s resulted in a series of critical, even damning pamphlets being published, yet immediately after his death there was little evidence of extreme assessments of him. After the restoration of monarchy in 1660, those who wrote about

Cromwell did so either to condemn his actions and put themselves in a good light, or to regret a lost opportunity, so criticism then became much more forceful.

Even two centuries after the death of Cromwell, it was impossible for historians to distance themselves from him. The British took pride in their parliamentary democracy, and the prevailing Whig view of history, with its emphasis on the inexorable progress towards the current constitutional system, influenced their interpretations of Cromwell. World events of the 1930s and 1940s led to a different approach. Comparing Cromwell with twentieth-century dictators, the American historian W. C. Abbott wrote, 'The rise of an Austrian house painter to the headship of the German Reich, of a newspaper editor-agitator to the leadership of Italy, and of a Georgian bandit to the domination of Russia, have modified our concept of Cromwell's achievement.' At the same time, Marxist interpretations portrayed Cromwell as the agent of a mid-seventeenth century bourgeois revolution. It is only relatively recently that historians have begun to examine Cromwell in the context of his time. However, this has not narrowed the range of opinion.

Cromwell's role in Ireland has also been manipulated to suit particular interpretations of history. The Irish Nationalist version condemns him, but recently historians have begun to seek out the evidence that will confirm or challenge this image of Cromwell.

Historians have also debated the legacy of the Interregnum. Again, different schools of historians have reached different conclusions, but there is now more unanimity. The particular interests of each historian – constitutional, social or cultural – can influence the conclusion, but there is agreement that Cromwell's legacy was limited. Roger Howell posed a number of questions in his 1977 biography of Cromwell. Was Cromwell a product of his time or did he rise above it and shape it? Did Cromwell change the course of history? These are the issues that historians have been examining in the last quarter century.

What was Cromwell's role in the execution of Charles I?

To monarchists and for those writing after the Restoration, the execution of the King was to be condemned. Cromwell's involvement in the decision to put Charles I on trial, and in the signing of his death warrant, rendered him a villain. What was his involvement in the sequence of events that led to this event?

Cromwell the mediator and negotiator

In April 1646, towards the end of the First Civil War, Charles I surrendered to the Scots. Parliament assumed he would bow to defeat and accept peace terms. In July Parliament offered him the Newcastle Propositions. Divisions then appeared in the Parliamentary side, with disagreements about what they wanted of the King. Well aware of this, Charles delayed making a firm reply to the proposals and began to make his own plans. These involved negotiations with the Scots to join him in a second civil war so that he could regain the initiative.

Cromwell was involved in two ways. Firstly, he had the difficult task of placating his soldiers. Parliament wanted to disband most of the Army, sending the remainder to Ireland to quell the continuing rebellion there. However, many soldiers were owed months' of pay. In the harsh economic climate of 1647, they were unwilling to be disbanded without guarantees regarding these arrears and without assurances that they would not be prosecuted for actions taken during the war. Elections took place among the soldiers for agitators and the General Army Council came into existence in June 1647. As a senior officer, or grandee, Cromwell was automatically on the Council. Debate about the future form of the constitution began, with the grandees' suggestion, the Heads of Proposals, put to the King by Cromwell. Herein lies Cromwell's second role – as a negotiator with the King.

The negotiations proceeded slowly, with the King, as ever, prevaricating. Cromwell had begun optimistically, and the King's responses had initially been encouraging. Meanwhile, the soldiers insisted on discussing new proposals based on Leveller ideas. The Army Council met at Putney Church in late October. In the debates, Cromwell did not put a coherent case for any particular constitutional form (see Chapter 2). However, it is clear that he had serious reservations about Charles's fitness as King. The debate continued for several days until news arrived of the King's escape from Army custody. There have been suggestions, although not adequately substantiated, that Cromwell engineered the escape bid in order to silence the Leveller-inspired soldiers. The King had eluded one of Cromwell's relations, Edward Whalley, only to be recaptured by another, Robert Hammond.

The road to regicide

Cromwell now doubted both the integrity of the King and the possibility of reaching a settlement with him. This was confirmed in December when it emerged that Charles's negotiations with the

The death warrant of King Charles I. Cromwell's signature (O Cromwell) is third down in the left-hand column.

parliamentary commissioners had been a smoke screen for talks with the Scots. In late December Charles signed an engagement with the Scots, leading to the Second Civil War. His captured correspondence further humiliated Cromwell and the Army grandees by showing that Charles had enjoyed fooling them. In January, Parliament voted to make no further addresses to the King.

In April 1648, at an Army prayer meeting at Windsor, Charles was referred to as 'that man of blood'. This was the signal that the Army was no longer prepared to contemplate him continuing as King. Cromwell was probably at the meeting. Certainly at some stage in 1648 Cromwell began to entertain the idea of putting the King on trial for treason, although historians are divided as to exactly when.

After Charles had lost the Second Civil War, Parliament voted to resume negotiations with the King, since the MPs could not find an alternative way forward. The Army lost patience, and on 6 December 1648 Colonel Pride purged Parliament of all those MPs sympathetic to the King.

In *Oliver Cromwell* (2001), Colin Davis states that, despite earlier claims, 'Few historians would now hold to the view that this was all engineered by an exceptionally cunning Cromwell'. Indeed, John Morrill and Philip Baker argue that this development left Cromwell in a quandary, since although by now he believed the King should be brought to account, he did want to do this legitimately. They argue that Cromwell only accepted that Parliament should put the King on trial after Charles and his two elder sons had refused even to propose their own terms for a settlement. Cromwell and others envisaged Charles's abdication and the succession of one of his three sons.

Once it was established that Charles would be tried, Cromwell showed complete commitment. One of the signatories on the death warrant later claimed that he had been forced to sign by Cromwell. However, in her memoirs of her husband's life, Lucy Hutchinson casts doubt on this story. 'Although some of them after, for excuse, belied themselves, and said they were under the awe of the army and overpersuaded by Cromwell, and the like, yet it is certain that all men herein were left to their own free liberty of acting, neither persuaded nor compelled.'

Cromwell's role in the execution, it seems, was to listen to all the arguments, consult his conscience and then show great commitment to what he believed was 'cruel necessity', that is, God's will. He was not proactive, he was 'a reluctant revolutionary', but he was not on the sidelines. He is a hero or a villain in this story depending on whether one agrees that the King's execution was the only realistic option.

What was Cromwell's role in the Irish campaign of 1649?

The Irish rebellion began in October 1641 and continued more or less unchecked until Cromwell was sent to join the Army there in August 1649. His campaign became notorious for the events at Drogheda and Wexford, involving the massacres of thousands of people. Historians such as David Stevenson have been keen to point out that, in comparison with contemporary commanders such as those of the Thirty Years' War (1618–1648), Cromwell was not particularly bloodthirsty.

The campaign was characterised by **siege warfare**, the most bloody and unforgiving of the time. Colin Davis summarises the range of opinions about Cromwell's role thus: 'The massacres of Drogheda and Wexford suggest to some the kind of viciousness we might now associate with what we could call 'war criminals'. For others, Cromwell represents a military discipline careful to minimise casualties and the impact of military activities on civilians; a commander of great compassion.'

Siege warfare: a military campaign in which soldiers surrounded a place to force the people inside to come out or surrender control. A siege could last a very long time if the defenders had plenty of supplies and the attackers were unable to breach the defences. At the end of a long siege, the victors were sometimes uncontrollable.

The siege of Drogheda

The siege of Drogheda ended with thousands of deaths. Reports range from two to four thousand. The sequence of events is difficult

to establish. By the rules of contemporary warfare, those who had surrendered should have been spared, but there was confusion about whether the defenders of the town had in fact surrendered. As historian Tom Reilly acknowledges: 'One cannot deny that whatever really happened at Drogheda can never now be accurately told; but with the use of eyewitness accounts and logical evaluation of all of the contemporary evidence, a discerning appraisal can now be made.' In *Cromwell: An Honourable Enemy* (1999), he concludes that Cromwell was not such a monster as some historians, particularly Irish Nationalist ones, have suggested. Nevertheless, Cromwell showed no remorse for what had happened. After the siege had ended, in September 1649, Cromwell wrote to Parliament, 'I am persuaded that this is a righteous judgement of God upon these barbarous wretches'.

The siege of Wexford

Events at Wexford are equally unclear. The town was full of soldiers, but few were native to the town. Many were killed by English soldiers fired up with bloodlust. However, this was not carried out on the orders of Cromwell or any other officers.

At both Drogheda and Wexford there were reports that civilians had died, but it is possible that these were civilians who had taken up arms to defend their town – as well they might in the circumstances. Suffice to say that Cromwell's unenviable reputation in Ireland stems from the unreliable accounts that circulated afterwards. Whatever the verdict, Colin Davis concludes that, 'Cromwell must be judged in the context of his own times and there were those who expected him to be much harsher in Ireland than he was'.

What happened after Cromwell left, had a far more lasting and damaging effect on the Irish. Great tracts of land were confiscated from the Anglo-Irish landowners. They, with their dependants, were resettled in the west while English soldiers were given their land. On the whole the native Irish tenants were not resettled, but the economic problems caused by war and major administrative changes led to great hardship. Peasants were reported to be eating grass and dying of starvation by the roadside. By 1660 the majority Catholic population owned only about 20% of the land and the population had dropped significantly.

Did Cromwell betray the English Revolution?

The answer to this final question depends on what is understood by the English Revolution. The aim here is simply to raise issues that can inform an assessment of Cromwell's legacy.

Political radicals

Barry Coward wrote 'if there ever has been an English Revolution it surely took place from December 1648 to January 1649'. This defines the revolution as a constitutional one, defined by the trial and execution of Charles I. Coward's subsequent chapter is entitled 'The failure of revolution, 1649–1660'. This suggests that, under Cromwell, there was a retreat from the extreme actions involved in executing the King and then abolishing both the monarchy and the House of Lords. This judgement is valid, in that the institutions of government came more and more to resemble those of the Stuart monarchy, even if Cromwell did reject the crown. Yet in terms of his policies, Cromwell did remain radical. It is the fact that he was realistic in the way he applied his beliefs that led some extremists to accuse him of betraying radical ideals.

If the political radicals (the Commonwealthsmen, Republicans and Levellers) are regarded as the true revolutionaries, then Cromwell is the villain. However, these radicals had misinterpreted Cromwell. They assumed that because he listened to, and agreed with, some of their ideas, he was 'on their side'. He was not. If his integrity is accepted, he neither used them nor betrayed them. They were simply sidelined by developments. This vocal minority had overestimated its influence. As Cromwell had earlier reminded the Army, it was the servant of Parliament. When mutiny threatened, Cromwell had to take action. This happened at Ware in 1647 and at Burford in 1649. Three soldiers were condemned to death at Ware – although only one was actually executed – and at Burford three of the 400 or so mutineers captured were shot in the churchyard. In fact, their protest was probably inspired by the fear that they were about to be sent to Ireland, rather than by Leveller ideas, but their mutiny coincided with vicious Leveller attacks in print on Cromwell as a betrayer of 'the cause'. The Levellers were challenging the legality of Charles's trial and execution as well as the legitimacy of the new regime, so Cromwell had no alternative.

Religious radicals

Of all the revolutionaries these, ultimately, were the winners. They

Landmark Study   **The book that changed people's views**

Christopher Hill, ***The World Turned Upside Down,*** Penguin, 1972

Until the twentieth century, the radicals of the English Revolution were almost forgotten. There were Chartist references to the legacy of the Levellers, but groups such as the Quakers tried to disassociate themselves from the more outrageous of their founders. The history of the seventeenth century was written with a 'top down' approach. This changed with the development of social history and the 'bottom up' approach, seeing the past from what Christopher Hill calls 'the worm's eye view'. Looking at the English Revolution from a wider perspective than the attack on monarchical authority, and that authority's subsequent restoration, led to a reassessment of the English revolution and hence of the role of Cromwell within it. Rather than focusing on Cromwell's contribution to the development of parliamentary democracy, historians became more aware of the significance of the diversity of ideas that developed and were published during the Interregnum. Hill sees this as a 'false dawn' of later radicalism. That we know about their ideas is a measure of the level of toleration under Cromwell. The radical revolutionaries were no more successful in the short term than the republican government, but the religious pluralism that the revolution gave rise to lived on.

had the opportunity to establish themselves as viable groups during the Cromwellian period. Many historians, including Barry Coward, regard the only tangible legacy of the Interregnum as 'the establishment of Protestant non-conformity as a permanent feature of life in Britain'.

Cromwell showed time and again that he aimed for far greater religious toleration than was acceptable to most people in the mid-seventeenth century. The degree of religious toleration permitted meant that not only did the numbers committed to religious sects grow enormously, but some of the sects established national organisations. As a result of this, when persecution struck during the Restoration period these sects were in a strong position to survive. For example, hundreds of the 60,000 or so Quakers who existed by 1660 were imprisoned in the various attacks on them during the reign of Charles II, yet their faith and organisation endured. If Cromwell had not remained firm in his belief that religious toleration was a non-negotiable fundamental of the constitution, then religious diversity would have been far less well placed to weather the storm of Restoration reaction. By the late 1680s, Cromwell's views were more widespread, and toleration of most non-conformist Churches was enshrined in law, but by then the national and international situation as well as changes in attitudes meant that relative toleration was politically acceptable.

Why is Cromwell seen as both a hero and a villain?

1. Read the following extract and answer the question.

> '*Cromwell's character remains very much an enigma, but it is clear that much of the praise lavished on him then and later is misplaced. In the early 1650s he alone stood between the English people and a peaceful permanent settlement; without his leadership and military genius, the republic would have foundered in its first two years; single-handed he postponed the inevitable restoration of monarchy for another ten. Moreover his increasing authoritarianism so weakened the cause for which he had struggled that after his death his bewildered and demoralised successors had to recall Charles II on his own terms. To the end he maintained his dignity, his sense of fairness, and above all his sense of humour; nevertheless, continued military victory, culminating in the 'crowning victory' of Worcester, gave him an undue confidence in the possession of God's grace.*'

(J. P. Kenyon, *Stuart England,* Penguin, 1985)

Using your knowledge of the period, how far do you agree with Kenyon's assessment of Cromwell?

2. To what extent do you agree with the Earl of Clarendon's interpretation of Cromwell as a 'brave bad man'?

Cromwell: an assessment

- Cromwell rose from relative obscurity and became Head of State reluctantly. As Head of State he only took on the trappings of office for the sake of appearances. In 1654 he told Sir Peter Lely, or possibly Samuel Cooper, to paint him 'warts and all', scorning the kind of image-making that had characterised early Stuart royal portraiture.

- No-one challenges the judgement that Cromwell was an effective army officer and a skilled military tactician.

- Cromwell was a man of his time, in terms of his political and religious concerns, but he had unusually tolerant attitudes towards other Protestants.

- Cromwell was not a political thinker, but he did have consistent principles.

- Cromwell was an Englishman of his time in his attitude to the Irish.

- Cromwell pursued a noble vision, often agonising over what course of action to take. He always tried to decide *what* was right, not *who* was right.

- Cromwell ruled the whole of the British Isles as one country, although his rule was very English dominated.

- The Cromwellian Protectorate was never a dictatorship; even though Cromwell clashed with his Parliament, he worked effectively with his Council and did not try to dominate it.

- His downfall lay in that promoting his vision for Britain was so expensive to enforce that insufficient civilian allies could be found for his regime.

- Cromwell did not achieve what he wanted, especially in terms of a godly reformation; he died a disappointed man.

- Within two years of his death the monarchy had been restored and before long draconian religious laws were introduced, persecuting the sects. However, non-conformity was not eliminated.

- It is difficult, perhaps impossible, to trace the modern concept of liberal democracy – with its constitutional monarchy, representative institutions and religious pluralism – to Cromwell's regime.

- Cromwell's reputation matters because he was a key figure at a time of great political and religious upheaval, stabilising and giving direction to government and reconciling many to his regime.

Cromwell's lying-in-state in Somerset House, London. A wax effigy was used, first lying, then raised to signify the passing of the soul to Heaven. The ceremony was closely modelled on that used for James I's lying-in-state.

Further reading

Texts specifically designed for students

Anderson, A. *The Civil Wars, 1640–9* (2nd edition, Hodder and Stoughton, 2003)

Lynch, M. *The Interregnum, 1649–60* (2nd edition, Hodder and Stoughton, 2002)

Texts for more advanced study

Coward, B. *Oliver Cromwell* (Longman, 1991 republished in 2000) is one of the standard recent biographies.

Coward, B. *The Cromwellian Protectorate* (Manchester University Press, 2002) provides a detailed account of the Protectorate and its legacy, along with selected documents and an extensive bibliography.

Davis, J. C. *Oliver Cromwell* (Arnold, 2001) provides a comprehensive critique of recent interpretations of Cromwell and arrives at conclusions that are sympathetic to Cromwell.

Gaunt, P. *Oliver Cromwell* (Blackwell, 1996) is a good, short biography assessing the man and the myth.

Hill, C. *God's Englishman* (Penguin, 1973) is a detailed account from a well-known Marxist historian.

Morrill, J. (ed) *Oliver Cromwell and the English Revolution* (Longman, 1990) is a book of indispensable essays, by a range of historians, covering all the main aspects of Cromwell's career and reputation.

Reilly, T. *Cromwell an honourable enemy* (Phoenix Press, 1999). Described by D. Smith as 'a provocative study', this book gives a sympathetic reassessment of Cromwell in Ireland.

Roots, I (ed) *Speeches of Oliver Cromwell* (Dent, 1989) contains Cromwell's most famous speeches, together with frequently-quoted conversations and some of his contributions to the Putney Debates.

Smith, D. *Oliver Cromwell: Politics and Religion in the English Revolution, 1640–1658* (Cambridge University Press, 1990 – currently out of print) is a useful collection of primary and secondary sources with commentary on the debate.

Smith, D. (ed) *Cromwell and the Interregnum* (Blackwell, 2003). A collection of scholarly essays covering important issues.

Index